ELI WHITNEY

ELI WHITNEY

JUDITH ALTER

Franklin Watts
New York   London   Toronto   Sydney
A First Book   1990

Cover photograph courtesy of: The Bettmann Archive

Photographs courtesy of: New Haven Colony Historical Society: pp. 2, 41, 55; Photo researchers: pp. 11 (Will McIntyre), 35 (Betsy Blass); The Bettmann Archive: pp. 13, 34, 48; Historical Picture Service: pp. 17, 21 bottom, 23, 30, 33, 43, 52; New York Public Library Picture Collection: pp. 20 top, 21 top, 26; Yale University Art Gallery: p. 45.

Library of Congress Cataloging-in-Publication Data

Alter, Judith, 1932-
    Eli Whitney/by Judith Alter.
        p.   cm. — (A First book)
    Includes bibliographical references.
    Summary: A biography of the inventor of the cotton gin, whose application of standardized parts to the production of weapons and other machines was a major influence in the development of industry.
    ISBN 0-531-10875-9
    1. Whitney, Eli, 1765-1825—Juvenile literature.   2. Inventors—United States—Biography—Juvenile literature.   [1. Whitney, Eli, 1765-1825.   2. Inventors.]   I. Title.   II. Series.
        TS1570.W4A47   1990
        609.2—dc20
    [B]   90-12222   CIP   AC

Contents

ELI WHITNEY

INTRODUCTION

Imagine for a moment that every car produced by a factory is slightly different—same make, same model, but none with parts that are exactly the same. Each car would have to be individually made, because assembly lines depend on parts that are all the same size and shape. Repairs would be a nightmare—parts would have to be made specifically for the car in question. It wouldn't be possible to simply order a new door, or a new steering column, or even a new headlight. Only uniformity makes parts interchangeable.

The nineteenth-century inventor Eli Whitney developed and put into practice the concept of standardized, interchangeable parts which is essential to American manufacturing today. Before his work, everything was individually made, each product slightly different. Whitney, working in the early 1800s to produce large quantities of muskets for the United States government, laid the groundwork for today's assembly lines, which produce identical cars, clocks, hardware, sewing machines, and a thousand other items. These products are made at a rapid rate and at far less cost than if each item were individually made by a skilled worker.

Today Eli Whitney is best known not for standardized parts but for his invention of the cotton gin—a machine which gins, or cleans, cotton bolls, removing cotton fibers from their seeds. (The word "gin" is probably a short form of the word "engine.") The invention of the cotton gin made cotton a major crop and created a textile manufacturing industry in the United States.

Today we use cotton for clothing, shelter, home furnishings, even food—cottonseed is rich in oil. The crushed hulls are used in plastics, horse and cattle feed, soil conditioners, synthetic rubber, and petroleum refining. The pressed kernels are used in fertilizers. Cotton linters (short fibers that stick to the seeds after ginning) are used in rocket fuel, toys, carpets, quilts, paints, hair-care products, toothpaste, and even in ice cream substitutes. Modern man is dependent on cotton, and it was Eli Whitney's invention of the cotton gin that made it more profitable to grow cotton. Without

Cotton yarn, here being inspected before leaving the textile plant, is one of the more obvious products developed from cotton.

the gin, cotton might never have become the major crop of the American South.

Whitney's two major accomplishments—the cotton gin and standardized parts—are really part of one big experiment. Whitney realized that no matter what was being manufactured, there was a need for a model which could be reproduced very closely in size and form. Precision was his goal; for example, each part in any musket had to exactly match the same part in every other musket.

Many people believe that inventions do not spring suddenly from one man's mind. They develop when the time is right and many men's minds are turned to similar problems. So it was with Eli Whitney and the cotton gin. Whitney lived during the Industrial Revolution, which changed forever the way people throughout the world earned a living. It was a time when inventors tinkered with machines, and their inventions made fac-

Like a revolution of any kind, the Industrial Revolution greatly affected people's lives. Eli Whitney was just one of the many inventors who worked with machines at this time.

tories possible. People left their farms to live in cities and work in these factories. They believed that machines had unlimited potential for making things. The Industrial Revolution, and the important change in lifestyle that it brought, began in England. But by the time Whitney was a young boy in Massachusetts, the effects of the Revolution had begun to reach the United States.

1

THE YOUNG ENTREPRENEUR

Eli Whitney was born December 8, 1765, in West-borough, Massachusetts. He was the oldest son of a farmer. He had one sister, Elizabeth, and two brothers, Benjamin and Josiah. As a young boy, he was a slow reader but quick with figures, and he loved to tinker with machines. Like most farmers, Eli's father had a workshop for making and repairing furniture and farm equipment, and Eli began his experiments there.

Once he claimed to be too sick to go to church. While the family was gone, he took his father's watch apart to see how it worked. By the time the family came home, he had it reassembled and running smoothly. At the age of twelve Eli made a violin, and by the Revolutionary War, he was ready to start a business. He suggested to his father that they install a forge and make nails, which were badly needed by the army. Business went so well that, without telling his father, he hired a workman. He figured it would not cost much to hire another man but it would increase profits considerably. The man worked for the Whitneys for three months. When peace ended the need for nails, Eli shifted to making hatpins and men's walking sticks, which he turned on the lathe his father kept for turning chair legs.

When he was nineteen, Eli decided he wanted to attend college. He had been working in the shop at the farm and had completed all the education his hometown had to offer. No one knows exactly what prompted him to seek more education, but he began to study for the difficult entrance exam to Yale University. The day-long test measured his knowledge of Latin and Greek and his understanding of English grammar and mathematics. He was twenty-three when he tried—and passed—the examination.

Whitney's years at Yale were difficult, for a college education cost a great deal of money. He was always short of money, although his father supported him the best he could. The schedule was also difficult—students were wakened at five-thirty in the spring and summer, at five in the fall and winter. They attended prayer service and recited lessons before breakfast at

Although his college life was difficult academically and financially, Eli Whitney prevailed. It wouldn't be the last time he would prove that hard work and dedication can solve the problem at hand.

eight, then studied in their rooms until eleven, when they again recited prepared lessons. After lunch and an hour of free time, they studied in order to recite again at four. The evening consisted of prayers, supper, and more study, all supervised by tutors.

Eli Whitney was conscientious and he studied hard, learning the scientific theories that made sense of his practical experience in his home workshop. He also learned to speak and write properly.

In the late summer of 1792, now nearly twenty-eight years old, Eli Whitney finished college. Although he planned to eventually study law, he needed to earn money immediately. A promised teaching position fell through, and he was advised to accept a position as a tutor to a family in South Carolina.

Eli Whitney was a New Englander and did not want to go to the South. "The climate is unhealthy and perhaps I shall lose my health and perhaps my life," he wrote to his brother. His journey south began by ship, and he was very seasick; then he contracted smallpox, though only a mild case. Eli Whitney was sure that bad luck had sent him to the South.

2

The Cotton Gin

While traveling, Eli met Mrs. Catherine Greene, widow of the Revolutionary War general Nathanael Greene, and Mr. Phineas Miller, who managed Mulberry Grove, the Greenes' large estate in Georgia. Whitney accepted their invitation to stop briefly at Mulberry Grove before continuing on to South Carolina. Whitney soon learned that he no longer had the job offer in South Carolina. Between this and the interesting developments at Mulberry Grove, he never got to South Carolina.

At Mulberry Grove he heard cotton planters discussing the problem of ginning cotton. There are two kinds of cotton: black seed (or long staple) and green seed (or short staple). Black seed was then grown in the West Indies and Brazil and was easily cleaned. Green

As cotton became more important to the southern states, plantation owners wanted more slaves to work the cotton fields. The dispute over slavery would ignite the Civil War.

seed, considered almost a weed, was the only kind that would grow in the interior land of the American South. Green seed was used only for coarse goods because it was nearly impossible to separate the fiber from the seeds. A slave could clean only a pound (less than half a kilogram) a day, which hardly made it profitable to grow cotton for export to the large textile mills in England.

Yet the South needed a basic crop. Farmers grew rice and indigo, but there was no profit in those, and tobacco wore out the soil. The planters Whitney met at Mulberry Grove insisted that a machine to clean cotton thoroughly and inexpensively would be "a great thing both to the country and to the inventor."

Eli Whitney had never even seen a cotton boll— the pod part of the plant that carries the seed, fiber, and linters—but he studied one and within a week came up with a small working model of a cotton gin. Miller, the Mulberry Grove manager, offered him money for the rights to his invention. Instead, they formed a partnership whereby Miller paid the expenses of Whitney's experiments to build a machine, in return for a share of the profits. Whitney spent the winter months working hard in a basement room at Mulberry Grove, and by June he had made the machine.

Whitney's gin cleaned ten times as much cotton as a man could clean in any other way, and it got the cotton much cleaner. He wrote to his father, "This machine

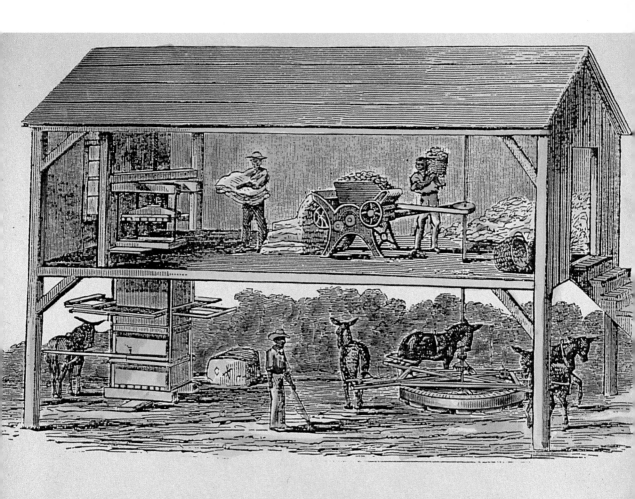

*Whitney's gin cleaned cotton better
than it had ever been cleaned before.
Suddenly, growing cotton was worth it!*

may be turned by water or with a horse, with the greatest ease, and one man and a horse will do more than fifty men with the old machines."

There had been gins before. They operated like an old-fashioned wringer washing machine, with two grooved wooden rollers which removed the seed by friction. But the seed of green seed cotton clung so tightly to the fibers that this method was not effective.

Whitney's machine used a revolving cylinder with hundreds of short wire hooks set at a carefully calculated angle. Opposite this cylinder was a grooved plate which held the seed while the cotton fibers, caught in the hooks, worked through. A second, smaller cylinder was set with bristles—Whitney said he got the idea from a hearth brush—and brushed the cleaned cotton out of the wire hooks. The inventor revealed that he used wire hooks instead of iron plates for teeth to hold the cotton simply because the material was handy— one of Mrs. Greene's daughters had some wire on hand for making a bird cage.

Phineas Miller and Catherine Greene urged Whitney to apply for a patent for the gin. Patent laws were new at that time. They supposedly made sure an inventor was the only one with the right to sell or use his machine or invention. Such laws had become necessary only because of the many inventions that came out of the Industrial Revolution. This advice convinced

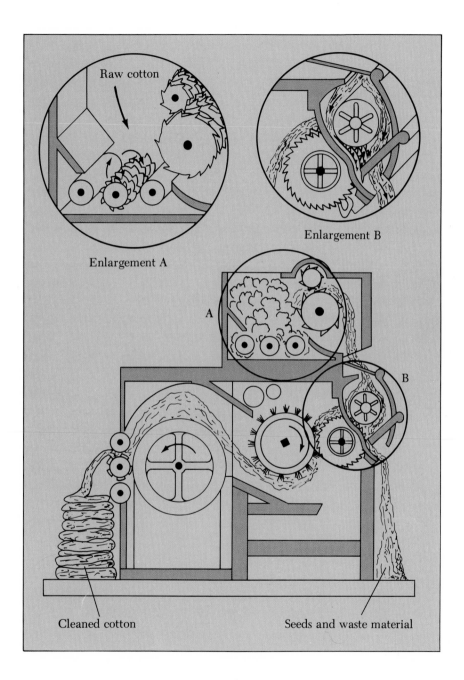

Raw cotton

Enlargement A

Enlargement B

A

B

Cleaned cotton

Seeds and waste material

Whitney that his cotton gin was important, and he wrote to his father, " 'Tis generally said by those who know anything about it that I shall make a Fortune by it."

With the cotton gin, Whitney had found his life's work. Teaching had not been something he was meant to do, and he had never really been drawn to law. In the spring of 1793 he was back in New England and hired several workmen to begin manufacture of the gin in a workshop in New Haven, Connecticut. He applied for a patent, but until the patent was granted he thought it best not to display the machine, for fear that others would copy it. Against his better judgment, Whitney had allowed Miller to display the working model to planters in Georgia. He would later regret that. Miller had also advertised in the *Georgia Gazette* that he would gin any quantity of green seed cotton; he gave this public notice, he said, to encourage the planters to put in a crop.

This cotton gin and carding machine, developed from Eli Whitney's invention, stands in front of the Whitney workshop.

Whitney and Miller recognized that they could never manufacture enough gins for every man who planted cotton; besides, most planters could not afford the price of four to five hundred dollars for a gin. The partners' solution was to establish a business that processed other men's cotton, with their fee paid not in cash but in cotton. There was little textile manufacturing in the United States, so there was no market for the ginned cotton at home, but there was a large British market. England had many textile factories which required great quantities of raw fiber.

3

BUSINESS PROBLEMS

Business was difficult for the partnership of Whitney and Miller. For Whitney, there were the problems of establishing the business—learning to deal with such things as packing, baling, and shipping the cleaned cotton. His plans did not proceed at the pace he had anticipated. One by one, he solved the problems he met, and all the while he kept a careful "Expence Book," recording every penny he spent for board, lodging, labor, and materials.

The patent was granted in 1794, and the cotton gin was called "the most perfect and valuable invention that has appeared in this country." But in 1795, a disastrous fire destroyed Whitney's workshop in New Haven, and he lost the parts for about twenty gins, along with the tools necessary for his manufacturing process. He had

*Facing page: Eli Whitney was granted
a patent for his cotton gin in March
of 1794. Patent laws were a new develop-
ment and thus were far from foolproof.*

E. Whitney.

Cotton Gin.

Patented Mar. 14, 1794.

NO PRINTED COPY OF SPECIFICATION IN OFFICE.

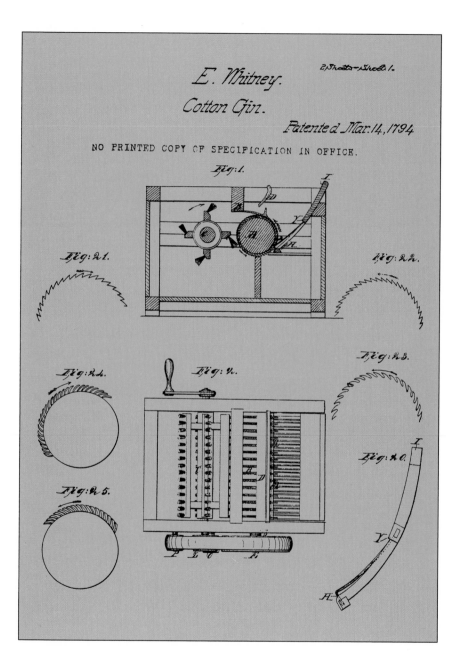

Fig: 1.

Fig: 21.

Fig: 22.

Fig: 24.

Fig: 23.

Fig: 4.

Fig: 20.

Fig: 25.

built lathes for his needs, and a wire-drawing block. He had also been working on a way to produce the gins more quickly, in quantity, and at fairly standard sizes and weights. Although the shop was rebuilt, the fire was a setback.

Cotton planters soon began to resent paying a high price to have their cotton ginned when, as they saw it, any mechanic could make the machine. Copycats began to put their own machines into use in spite of the patent law. Some claimed that they operated under patents granted to improvements on Whitney's original model, but Whitney's patent had especially stated that such new patents would not be granted. He himself was constantly improving the original design with new ideas like a bagging machine.

The cotton the partnership took in as payment was shipped to England, as Whitney and Miller had planned. But British spinners were reluctant to buy the ginned green seed cotton because its fiber length was different from that of the cotton they usually worked with—black seed. Resentful Southern planters started a rumor that the gin ruined cotton, and British spinners believed it and did not buy the cotton. Without the British market, Whitney and Miller had nowhere to sell their ginned cotton. At the end of 1796, it seemed that the business had failed, and with it went Whitney's dreams of wealth and security.

The expanding cotton industry also gave rise to a growth in the shipping industry. All that nice clean cotton had to be sent somewhere to be used.

Ginning cotton has come a long way
from its beginning. What was originally
a project requiring at least two people can
now be done automatically by machines.

Whitney and Miller had learned the bitter lesson that a patent does not protect an invention; it simply gives the patent owner the right to sue someone who copies their invention. There were many copycats making cotton gins, but Whitney and Miller sued the major offender, Edward Lyon of Georgia. The decision went against them, mostly because the patent law was so new that it had big loopholes in it. By 1798, they had cotton gins but no cotton to clean.

Miller decided on a new business policy and announced that they would sell gins, lease them, or sell the rights to manufacture the machines. Things began to look a little more hopeful. Toward the close of the century, a new patent law was passed that gave strength to the claims of Whitney and Miller, and they again sued their competitors. State legislators in South Carolina paid fifty thousand dollars for the rights to use Whitney's invention, and North Carolina and Tennessee followed. The one state that refused to treat the inventor fairly was Georgia, the state in which the gin had been invented. Whitney and Miller did not win their case there until 1807—too late for Phineas Miller to enjoy the victory; he had died in 1803.

Whitney and Miller might have had less trouble with their business if they had been better businessmen. Without meaning to, the two partners arranged their business so that they had a monopoly on ginning cotton, and the planters who rebelled did so out of financial necessity because they could not afford the high prices.

For Eli Whitney, the invention of the cotton gin was a mixed blessing. The patent expired in 1807, and he was unable to extend it. The way was clear for others to manufacture and use his invention. He did not gain the great wealth that he had expected. Like many inventors, he found that his invention brought more wealth to others than to himself. Later it would be suspected that the long, difficult legal problems had damaged his health. And the most unhappy part was that Whitney came to believe that the United States did not value its inventors.

Yet the cotton gin did more than earn Whitney a place in history; it was also a learning experience for him. Manufacturing the gins taught Whitney the techniques and organization he would use in a new project.

Equally important, the cotton gin had a major impact on the United States. In the South, previously unemployable people such as the young and the old found work because they could operate the gins without having great strength; debts were paid; land increased in value. The North benefited too, for now it had raw materials for its factories and cargo for its ships.

In the rest of the world . . .

1746–1828   Francisco José de Goya y Lucientes, Spanish painter.

1770–1850   William Wordsworth, English poet.

1775–1817   Jane Austen, English novelist.

1784   First American ship reaches China.

1789   George Washington becomes first president of the United States.
The French Revolution begins.

1793   Eli Whitney invents the cotton gin.
The Louvre becomes a national art gallery in Paris.
Louis XVI and Marie Antoinette are executed in France.

1793–1794   Reign of Terror in France under Robespierre.

1794   First telegraph invented, Paris to Lille.

1796   Edward Jenner introduces a small-pox vaccine.

4

STANDARDIZED PARTS

Whitney had turned his attention to a new project in the late 1790s, almost ten years before the final decisions in the cotton gin cases. Very depressed by the legal battles, he had withdrawn from the affairs of Whitney and Miller and left most of the legal and business responsibility to Miller.

But Eli Whitney was too creative a person to remain sunk in depression for long. Soon his isolation turned into creativity, and his mind was busily seeking a new project. His basic need was for money to finance a new project. His relationship with Miller had taught him that it was dangerous to be dependent on the patronage of one man of wealth, and he decided that he would do business with the federal government. There were, he thought, big advantages to doing business with a single buyer.

Whitney wrote to Secretary of the Treasury Oliver Wolcott, proposing a machine for making screws, but the idea had already been suggested by someone else. Next, he proposed to supply between ten and fifteen thousand muskets to the government.

Eli Whitney had never made a musket, but after all, he had known little about cotton when he invented the gin. Familiarity with a musket was not important to him; he believed that the basic manufacturing process, with which he was now highly familiar, could be used to build any object needed.

Muskets were particularly needed just before the close of the eighteenth century. Muskets for the Revolutionary War had come from France, but by the late 1790s the United States found itself facing probable war with France, the country on which it depended for arms.

Manufacture of arms in the United States was slow. The U.S. armory at Springfield produced less than one thousand muskets in its first three years—hardly enough to equip an army. Each musket was handmade, with the maker depending on his hands and eyes to judge the accuracy of the size of the parts. The parts of an individual musket were fitted together by hand, and each varied from the next. Whitney proposed to re-

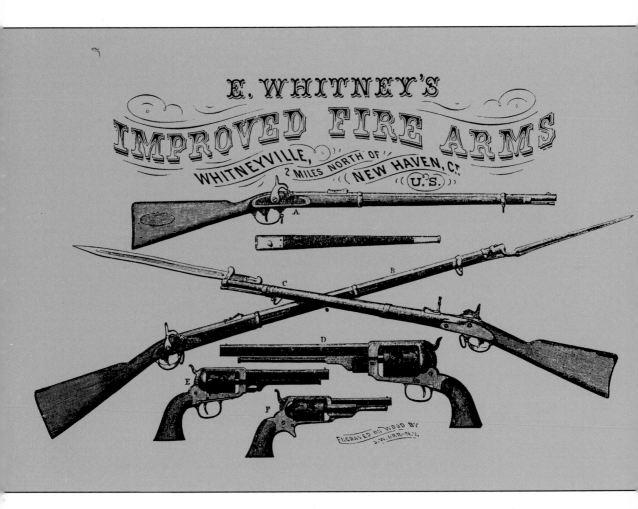

*This ad from the early 1800s states
that Whitney's rifles were balanced,
warranted, durable, and recommended by
Kit Carson and Colonel Jefferson Davis.*

place these handmade arms with mass-produced, standardized muskets, to be produced thousands at a time.

Whitney was given a contract for ten thousand stands of arms. A stand was the musket, the bayonet, the ramrod for ramming a charge down the muzzle, the wiper, and the screwdriver. They were to be made within slightly over two years, the first four thousand to be delivered by September 1799. No one thought he could do it, but Whitney was in a hurry to establish himself and the government was anxious to have arms, so the contract was signed. At the same time, the government gave contracts to other armories where workmen would make stands of arms by the traditional method.

Whitney's system was to break the musket into parts and then design and invent a machine to turn out each part. Previously men had thought in terms of one machine to make one product—a machine to make a musket, for instance. Machines were already making simple things, but this was a pioneer use of the new technology to make a complicated item. Whitney faced the challenge of designing machines to replace the handwork of skilled craftsmen.

Many Americans were working on labor-saving devices at the same time, but the United States was still a country of scattered, small towns, and communication was slow. Each inventor worked almost in isolation.

*This rifling machine would help
to produce uniform muskets.*

Whitney knew that others were working on the same idea, and he never claimed to have invented standardized parts. After the cotton gin, he never again attempted to patent anything, even the machines he used to make parts for muskets.

Because he needed water to power his machines, Whitney's first step was to choose a mill site at Mill Rock, near New Haven, Connecticut. He established his Mill Rock workshop at a place where a 35-foot (10.7-m) waterfall provided plenty of power for the mill. When a second arms factory, to be run by a competitor, was proposed nearby to centralize arms production at New Haven, Whitney successfully objected; the cotton gin had taught him the dangers of competing for labor and raw materials.

Once again, Whitney had problems: an early snowstorm and a bitter winter delayed construction of the workshop, yellow fever in Philadelphia meant quarantine of the iron and steel he needed, and there was financial difficulty in spite of his government backing. Finally, there was still doubt that he could accomplish what he said. Secretary of the Treasury Wolcott supported him, but others suggested that perhaps he was merely bragging.

Two years after the contract was signed, Eli Whitney still had not produced a musket. With three months to go before his first deadline, Whitney was

*Eli Whitney's mill site was soon
a village unto itself, including housing
for all the men who worked there.*

granted an extension. In spite of the extension, many thought he was a failure. Most manufacturers are judged by their results, and Whitney had not produced one musket, although he had many parts stacked in his shop. Today, familiar with the basic idea of mass production, we recognize those stacks of parts as progress, but to the people of the late 1700s they meant nothing. What mattered was that Eli Whitney was known as an honest and dependable man. When the terms of the extension included that, should he fail, he must be able to return the ten-thousand-dollar advance he had received to begin work, several prominent citizens of New Haven agreed to underwrite the debt. For Whitney, it was a vote of confidence from people of some importance.

5

DELAYED SUCCESS

Trouble loomed again for the business in 1801. The government was about to change hands. President John Adams had been voted out in the election of 1800, and Thomas Jefferson would be taking office. Jefferson was not only an intellectually curious man, but he had some knowledge of arms manufacture in France—and he had long ago corresponded with Whitney about the cotton gin.

Still, Whitney thought it necessary to travel to Washington to convince the new government of the importance of his work. At a meeting before those leaving office and those coming in, he displayed parts of locks (one part of a musket) and muskets in piles on the table. Drawing at random from each pile, he assembled a lock; then he let the others do it. Doing, as well as

Long before Thomas Jefferson was president, he had expressed hope in Whitney. He would turn out to be a faithful supporter of Eli's work.

seeing, convinced them of the project's progress, and Whitney was given more money and another extension on his deadline.

By the spring of 1801 the factory was running smoothly and the system working. Whitney delivered his first five hundred muskets in September of that year, and his advice was sought as an expert on arms.

The U.S. did not go to war with France after all, so the need for muskets was not so urgent. Whitney's twenty-eight-month contract was stretched over a period of ten years. He fulfilled his contract in 1809. Although he delivered all the muskets required, he made little profit. Still, he was able to pay his debts, and he owned the shop and machines at Mill Rock.

In 1808 government orders for stands of arms stopped. Whitney had assumed they would continue indefinitely. But the government had national armories, and could save money by producing weapons in its own factories. Whitney had to turn to private customers. That year, too, the secretary of war claimed to have found flaws in Whitney's muskets; the inventor protested that his workmen would never be careless. Paid by the day instead of by the piece, they had nothing to gain by rushing to produce more pieces. Whitney was right—the flaws were in the iron; no process had yet been developed to detect weaknesses in the metal.

Collection of damages from those who had violated his cotton gin patent eased Whitney's financial burden during these years. He had invested wisely, so money was not the problem when he lost contracts. His life's work, to which he had devoted all his energy, was at stake, and he was determined to keep the shop at Mill Rock open. He felt his professional reputation was at stake, and besides that, he was aware that his workmen depended on him.

Even though he had clearly established that his system worked, there were continually voices of doubt. The idea was too new for some to accept, and Whitney became preoccupied with seeing it accepted. He was always improving his system and his designs, and was always caught in the midst of political battles that threatened his business. But, generally, he was recognized as an engineer and an industrialist, and he was securely enough established that he received government contracts for various projects other than stands of arms. Then the War of 1812 brought renewed arms contracts from the government.

6

THE FINAL YEARS

For much of his adulthood, Eli Whitney's work was his whole life. He had no existence beyond it, though honors and friends came his way. In 1795, when the cotton gin business was at its lowest point, he received an honorary master of arts degree from Yale University. In later years he was a charter member of the Connecticut Academy of Arts and Sciences and a member of the United States Military Philosophy Society. He counted President Thomas Jefferson among his friends, and Jefferson repeatedly expressed his faith in Whitney when the production of muskets was in doubt.

But Eli Whitney had no wife and family. In the years when he manufactured cotton gins, he literally lived in his workshop. When he established his musket factory at Mill Rock, he was practically the overseer of a

small village. He built houses on the property for his workmen with families and a boardinghouse for the single men. He himself lived in a noisy house filled with young apprentices and three nephews whom he was raising and educating. A wealthy man late in his life, he was also generous with both his time and money.

Whitney had always wanted to marry but had not had time to meet and court a suitable wife. He remained single until 1817 when, at the age of fifty-two, he married thirty-one-year-old Henrietta Edwards, the daughter of a friend. Whitney left no diaries or personal records, so we do not know much about their courtship or their life together.

Eli and Henrietta had four children, and the death of one in infancy was a great tragedy for them. But Eli Whitney was not destined to enjoy family life for long.

Eli Whitney was a well-respected man. He earned people's respect not only by his inventions, but also by giving generously of himself.

Nearly all his life he had suffered periods of ill health. The earliest came even before he entered Yale. It was probably caused by the stress of earning money for his education and at the same time studying for the stiff entrance examination. Repeated illnesses during his professional life were probably the result of the pressures he felt in his work.

But in 1820 Whitney's health grew worse, and he was diagnosed as suffering from an incurable condition that affected his ability to urinate. Even worse, there was no known way to relieve the intense suffering that went with it. Whitney began to study everything he could about the disease, and eventually he invented an instrument which relieved his pain and no doubt prolonged his life by several years.

Eli Whitney died in 1825, a man of importance in his community and his country. His own sons were still small children, and it was left to his nephews to carry on his work. One—Eli Blake—had apparently inherited his uncle's creativity and later invented a rock crusher for use in road building that is much like the one used today. In the hands of Whitney's heirs, the Mill Rock armory was one of the country's leading private manufacturers of weapons for nearly a hundred years.

Just as cotton brought new life to the South, Whitney's muskets gave the industrial North new power by establishing the machine tool industry.

*The Whitney Armory was on the banks of
the Mill River near New Haven, Connecticut.*

*   *   *

Eli Whitney had been sure that it was bad fortune when he lost his prospective tutoring position in South Carolina. But that twist of fate proved to be the mischance upon which his career was built. If he had not gone to Mulberry Grove in Georgia, he would never have known of the need for an efficient cotton gin. And though the cotton gin brought him little or no money, caused him years of financial and emotional stress, and probably ruined his health, it gave him a professional career and taught him the lessons he needed to be successful as a manufacturer of muskets.

The importance of Whitney's work goes beyond a well-made musket. Because he was always more interested in the system of production than the product manufactured, he is called the father of the American system of interchangeable manufacturing.

FOR FURTHER READING

Feldman, Anthony. *Scientists and Inventors*. New York: Facts on File, 1979.

Green, Constance M. L. *Eli Whitney and the Birth of American Technology*. Boston: Little, Brown & Company, 1956.

Olmsted, Denison. *Memoir of Eli Whitney*. Reprint of 1846 edition. New York: Arno Press, 1972.

Vialls, Christine. *The Industrial Revolution Begins*. Minneapolis, Minn.: Lerner Publications, 1982.

GLOSSARY

Cotton boll: the rounded pod or seed portion of the cotton plant

Cotton gin: a machine for separating the cotton fibers from the seed of the plant

Forge: to form a metal object by heating, or hammering the metal when heated

Interchangeable: parts that can be put or used in place of each other; parts that can be replaced with each other

Lathe: a machine for working metal or wood that rotates the metal or wood against a tool that shapes it; for instance, the leg of a chair may be given ridges and curves in a lathe

Locks: in firearms, the mechanism that explodes the gunpowder or charge

Manufacturing: the process of creating goods by hand labor or by machinery; the making of a thing

Mischance: bad luck

Musket: a heavy, old-fashioned handgun, predecessor of the modern rifle

Stand of arms: an old-fashioned term for the complete set of arms given to any one soldier

Smallpox: a highly contagious disease characterized by small red sores on the skin, which often leave permanent scars

INDEX

About The Author

Judy Alter lives in Texas and writes mostly about the American West. Her books include *Women of the Old West,* a first reader describing the lives of many different women in the Old West; *Growing Up in the Old West,* another first reader detailing what life was like for children in the days of the wagon train and the sod hut; and many works of fiction.

Ms. Alter lives in Fort Worth, Texas; she is the mother of four teenagers.